EXTREME BIOLOGY

Creeping Killers

Extreme Plants

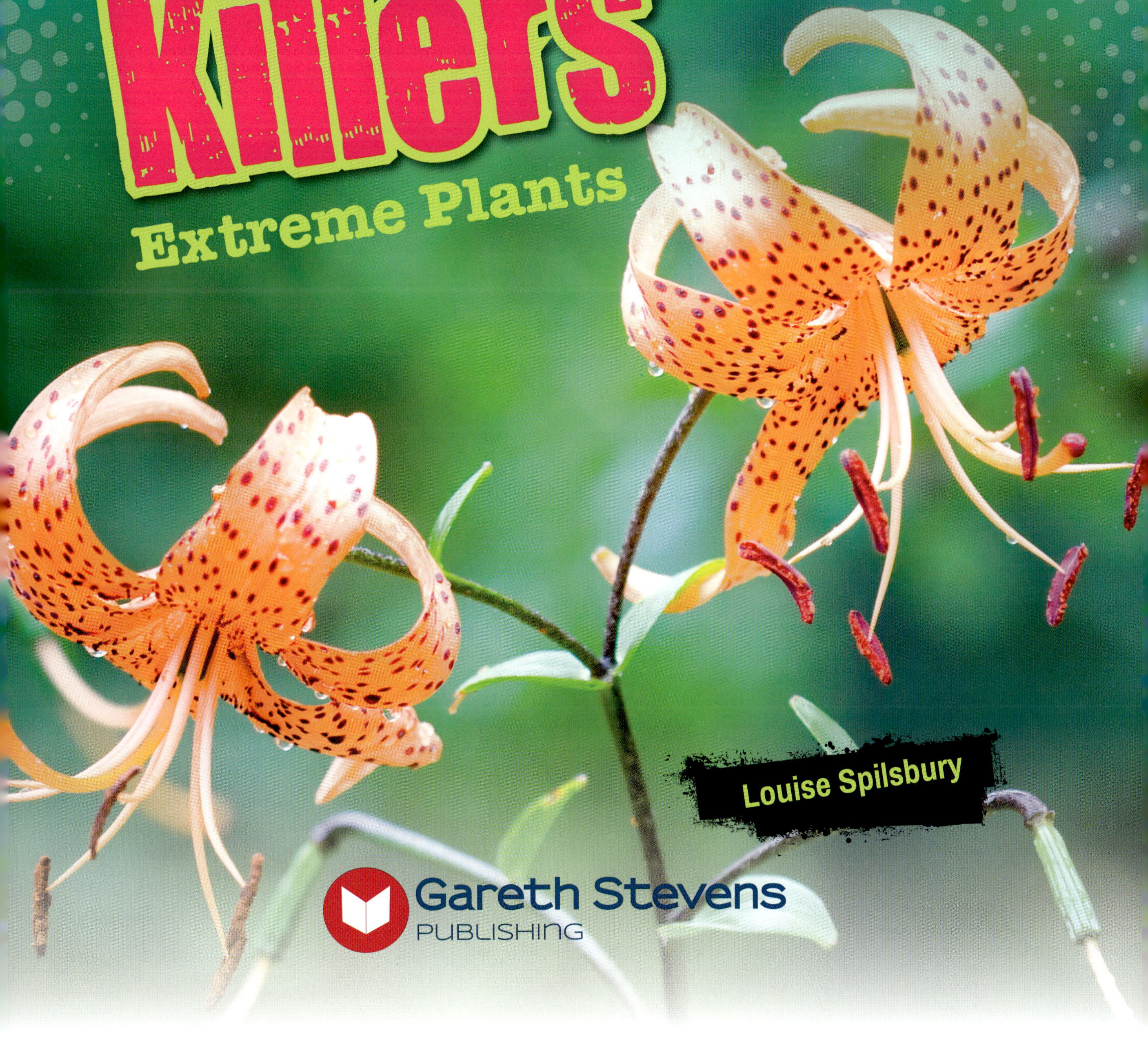

Louise Spilsbury

Gareth Stevens
PUBLISHING

Please visit our website, **www.garethstevens.com**. For a free color catalog of all our high-quality books, call toll free 1-800-542-2595 or fax 1-877-542-2596.

Library of Congress Cataloging-in-Publication Data
Spilsbury, Louise, author.
Creeping killers : extreme plants / Louise Spilsbury.
pages cm. — (Extreme biology)
Includes bibliographical references and index.
ISBN 978-1-4824-2236-8 (pbk.)
ISBN 978-1-4824-2237-5 (6 pack)
ISBN 978-1-4824-2234-4 (library binding)
1. Plants—Adaptation—Juvenile literature. 2. Carnivorous plants—Juvenile literature.
3. Poisonous plants—Juvenile literature. 4. Plant defenses—Juvenile literature.
I. Title.
QK921.S65 2015
581.4—dc23
2014027584

First Edition

Published in 2015 by
Gareth Stevens Publishing
111 East 14th Street, Suite 349
New York, NY 10003

Produced by: Calcium, www.calciumcreative.co.uk
Designed by: Paul Myerscough
Edited by: Sarah Eason and John Andrews
Picture research by: Rachel Blount

Photo credits: Cover: Shutterstock: Cathy Keifer; Inside: Dreamstime: Adimud71 22, John Anderson 37, Linda Bair 21, Halil I. Inci 41, Kuponjabah 42, Kzenia 39, Rico Leffanta 31, Fabio Lotti 28, Uriah Mosin 10, Noreen303 16, Sdbower 11, David Steele 24, Wallaceweeks 34; Shutterstock: AlessandroZocc 7, BMJ 8, Charles Brutlag 17, Chrislofotos 26, Dimijana 40, Belozorova Elena 12, Karen Hermann 32, Cathy Keifer 4, Daleen Loest 13, Elena Mirage 23, Dmitry Naumov 19, Plasid 3, 44, Lee Prince 35, Dr. Morley Read 20, Sue Robinson 14, Nicram Sabod 5, Santibhavank P 43, Bernd Schmidt 36, Kuttelvaserova Stuchelova 45, Diana Taliun 38, Marco Uliana 6, Evlakhov Valeriy 33, Birute Vijeikiene 1, 18, Bildagentur Zoonar GmbH 15, 27; Wikimedia Commons: Gnangarra 25, Pharaoh Han 29, Michal Rubeš 9, Mar del Sur 30.

Printed in the United States of America

CPSIA compliance information: Batch #CW15GS: For further information contact Gareth Stevens, New York, New York at 1-800-542-2595.

Contents

Chapter 1

Flesh-Eating Plants

Most of the plants we see around us work in much the same way, but there are some that break all the rules. These plants have extreme features or behaviors to help them survive, reproduce, or get food. Carnivorous, or flesh-eating, plants are a great example. Most plants make their own food from sunlight and air using a process called photosynthesis. Carnivorous plants get some of the nutrients they need to live by eating insects and other small animals.

The Not-So-Sunny Sundew

The sundew sounds like such a pleasant plant—but don't be fooled! This plant lives in wet, sometimes sandy, places where it cannot get all the nutrients it needs from the soil. So, to survive, a sundew resorts to more devious means. The plant catches and digests small animals such as insects to supplement its poor diet.

The substance on the sundew's leaves that attracts insects to the plant also traps them.

A Sticky End

Insects that come near a sundew plant meet a sticky end. Sundews have hairs covering their leaves, which work like sticky flypaper. Once an insect is stuck to the hairs, it cannot escape. The hairs slowly curl up and wrap themselves around their prey. Eventually, the whole leaf wraps around the prey, and the insect victim is slowly digested and absorbed by the plant.

Extra Extreme

In Australia, there is a sundew plant that has some extra long hairs that stretch out like tentacles around the edge of the leaf. When these hairs sense an insect, they flip or catapult the creature into the center of the leaf, where it is trapped on the sticky hairs and digested.

Sundews were named for the way the sticky hairs on their leaves glisten like dew.

Venus Flytrap

The Venus flytrap is the deadly plant that has inspired many horror movies about dangerous, man-eating plants! The real Venus flytrap does not eat people, but it has an awesome way of catching flies and other prey.

Jaws of Death

The leaves of the Venus flytrap are shaped in an amazing way to form a trap. At the end of each leaf, there is a folding part that can open and close like jaws. There are 14 to 20 spikes sticking out from the edges of this trap, and on the surface inside the leaves, there are tiny hairs that work like triggers. If an insect lands on a leaf and touches two of these hairs within a short space of time, the leaf closes and the spikes form a cage from which the insect cannot escape.

A Venus flytrap can shut its trap in the blink of an eye.

Eaten with Enzymes

After the plant has caught an insect, the trap closes tighter and tighter to squash the prey. The plant also makes a sticky substance to seal the gaps around the edge, where the two sides of the trap meet. Then it releases special substances called enzymes that break down the prey's body into pieces small enough for the plant to absorb. A few days later, after the insect has been digested, the trap reopens, ready for another victim.

Each trap on a Venus flytrap only works three or four times. Then it dies back or simply starts to make its food by photosynthesis, like most other leaves.

Extra Extreme

The Venus flytrap does not only eat insects. Sometimes even small frogs get trapped in its fast-moving, toothed leaves.

Bladderwort

In a lake, bog, or stream near where you live, there might be a quick-fire killer plant floating in the water. The bladderwort plant gets its name from tiny pouches called bladders that grow out of its stem. The plant sucks tiny prey into the bladders with extreme force to get the nutrients it needs.

Preparing the Weapons

Bladders on a bladderwort are hollow chambers with a flexible door. The plant gets the bladders ready for action by emptying the water out of them. This makes the pressure inside the bladders much lower than the surrounding water, which creates sucking power.

Bladderworts need to catch extra food because they live in clean freshwater that does not have many nutrients in it.

Bladderworts float because they have hollow stems. They do not need roots because they get nutrients from the water around them.

Triggering Death

Tiny hairs at the opening of the bladder are like triggers. A passing water flea or other animal creates small currents in the water that make the hairs move. Then the bladder door suddenly opens, the passing prey is sucked in, and the door closes again in an instant. The door seals around the prey, even if it is part of a larger animal, such as a polliwog's leg or tail. Any part of a prey animal trapped in a bladder is slowly digested.

Extreme!

In the Blink of an Eye!

Bladderworts are some of the fastest plants in the world. The door of a bladder can open and close in about a millisecond. There are 1,000 milliseconds in a second. That means the bladderwort moves too quickly for the human eye to see.

Pitcher Plant

Tropical pitcher plants are cunningly carnivorous, devouring insects that fall into their deep, deadly traps. These plants are named for the hollow structures at the tips of their leaves, which are shaped like pitchers with open lids. Any insect that falls inside a pitcher ends up as a meal.

Attracting a Meal

These merciless killer plants attract visiting insects first with the bright purple and pink colors of their pitchers. However, it is the smell of sweet nectar made in glands under the pitcher lid that really excites the insects. Some pitcher plants lace their nectar with chemicals that slow the insects down. They are then more likely to stumble to their doom.

The pitcher has a lid that acts like an umbrella to stop rain filling it up. Rain could make the pitcher so heavy that it breaks off the leaf.

Most pitcher plants lure insects, but some trap bigger prey, such as frogs.

Death Slide

Pitcher plants make sure their victims can never escape once they have been trapped. The lip of the pitcher leaf is covered with downward-pointing hairs that stop insects from climbing out of the top. Below the lip, the walls of the pitcher are smooth, hairless, and waxy. Any insect trying to get a grip scrambles and plunges down as if on a greased death slide! The prey falls into a pool of liquid at the bottom of the pitcher and drowns. Then, enzymes turn the unfortunate creature into a liquid lunch.

Extra Extreme

The largest pitcher plant in the world rarely traps prey. Instead, small mammals called tree shrews perch on the lip of the 12-inch- (30-cm) wide pitcher, feed on the nectar, and then poop inside. The plant gets its vital nutrients from the animal's waste.

Chapter 2

Toxic Terrors

Many plants contain toxins, or poisons, for defense. They can harm animals that try to eat them or even just touch them. Some of these plants are poisonous to people too and can make us sick—or even kill us. Such cases are rare, but once you read about some of these nasties of nature, you will know why it is best not to eat anything straight from a plant or bush.

Doll's Eyes Plant

This strange wildflower reaches up to 3 feet (90 cm) high. Some people grow it in their backyards for its distinctive fruits. The plant is called "doll's eyes" because the shiny white berries that appear at the top of its thick, blood-red stems have small dark spots on the ends, which make them look like the china eyes once used in dolls.

All parts of the doll's eyes plant are extremely poisonous if eaten.

Deadly Fruits

The berries might look like they come from a doll, but they contain deadly toxins. In fact, most animals know to leave the plant alone to avoid certain death. The berries from the doll's eyes plant are so poisonous that as few as five or six can make you very sick—eating any more could kill you. However, the fruit tastes so bad that most people never try more than one berry.

Extra Extreme

Amazingly, birds are immune to the toxins in doll's eyes berries and can eat them without being harmed. The toxins do not harm the birds because the plant wants birds to eat its berries. Then, when the birds poop out the seeds that were inside the fruits, the seeds can grow somewhere new.

The eye-like berries of the doll's eyes plant look like they are watching you!

Deadly Nightshade

The name "deadly nightshade" is a clear warning to avoid this dangerous plant! The toxic terror grows in the shade of trees in woods or on wastelands, and its shiny black berries are its weapons of choice.

Packed with Poisons

The deadly nightshade plant can grow as high as 6 feet (2 m) tall, and it has deep-purple or deep-blue flowers with orange or yellow stamens—the stalks in the middle of the flowers. The stem, leaves, berries, and roots of this plant contain poisons called atropine and scopolamine. However, it is the berries that are truly lethal. They taste so sweet that they tempt animals to eat them—at their peril. The poisons the berries contain paralyze muscles inside the body, including the heart.

Deadly nightshade is deadly to humans and some animals, but birds eat the berries, and horses, rabbits, and sheep feed on the leaves without getting hurt.

Making Medicine

The species name for deadly nightshade contains the word "belladonna," which means "beautiful woman" in Italian. There is a legend that long ago some women in Italy were foolish enough to eat deadly nightshade because it made the pupils of their eyes widen, which they thought made them look more beautiful. This was highly dangerous, and no one would ever do that today. However, people have used extracts of the atropine poisons in deadly nightshade to make a medicine that helps doctors widen patients' pupils for eye surgery.

Just two berries can kill a child and 10 could kill an adult.

Extreme!

Deadly Dinners?

Did you know that some of the foods we eat come from plants closely related to deadly nightshade? We can happily eat tomatoes, chili peppers, and cooked potatoes or eggplants, but we should never eat the leaves from those plants as they contain toxins that can be harmful.

Snakeroot

A native plant of North America, snakeroot was named for the mistaken belief among early settlers in the United States that its roots could help cure people who had been bitten by snakes. Rather than helping people, this plant is another toxic terror.

Death in the Fields

Snakeroot flower heads are several inches across and contain many white flowers that produce black seeds with small tufts of white hair. These hairs act like silken parachutes that carry seeds away on the wind, so snakeroot plants spread far and wide. To stop animals from eating it, the snakeroot plant contains a lethal toxin known as trematol. When livestock such as cattle, horses, goats, and sheep come across this plant at the edge of a field and eat too much of its leaves and roots, they can die.

Cattle, horses, and sheep are the animals most often poisoned by snakeroot.

Snakeroot plants can spread quickly and far and wide.

Milk Sickness

When cattle and sheep eat snakeroot, their meat and milk become contaminated with the plant's toxins. Calves and lambs may die from drinking their mothers' milk even if the amount of poison inside a mother's body is not enough to harm the parent. If humans drink milk or eat beef from cattle contaminated with snakeroot poisons, they get a condition called milk sickness, which can kill them too.

Extra Extreme

When settlers first arrived in the United States, they did not know about the dangers of snakeroot. Many thousands were killed by milk sickness. Its best-known victim was President Abraham Lincoln's mother, who is believed to have died from milk sickness in 1818. She was only 34 years old.

Lethal Lily

Animal charities have issued public warnings about lily plants. People put lily plants in their backyards and buy lily flowers in their bouquets, but these decorative plants can kill some of our favorite pets.

A Killer in Disguise

People often buy lilies because these flowers look exotic and are strongly scented, filling a home with a sweet perfume. However, several types of lily, such as Easter lily, tiger lily, and rubrum lily, bring something else into our homes as well—poisons that are deadly to cats. If a cat eats even a small amount of a lily, it can prove fatal. The toxin damages the animal's kidneys, and if a cat that has consumed part of a lily is not rushed to the vet within six hours, it can die.

Lily pollen looks like a fine dust on the long, oblong stamens in the center of a lily flower.

Some bunches of lilies come with a health warning that they are dangerous to cats.

Poisoned Pollen

Every part of the lily plant—the leaf, stem, and flower—is poisonous, but the pollen contains the highest concentration of toxins. Pollen is a fine powder found on the stamens that stand up like tiny stalks in the center of a flower. Cats can be affected by pollen if some falls on their fur or they brush up against lily flowers. When a cat licks and grooms its fur later, it may also swallow a fatal dose of the poisonous powder.

Extra Extreme

The stunning Easter lily, with its trumpet-shaped, white flowers, is a native of Japan. A soldier named Louis Houghton first brought it to the United States. He carried some of the bulbs home with him when he returned from Japan after serving in World War I.

Chapter 3

Parasitic Plants

Parasites are living things that exist on or in other living things, known as hosts. They do not just hitch a ride but also steal from the thing they live on or in, usually by taking its food. In the process, parasites can weaken or harm the host, but usually not enough to kill it. Otherwise, where would their next meal come from?

Dodder is a type of parasitic plant that grows into and grasps other plants.

Takeout Food

Most parasitic plants tap into their host's stems, where supplies of water with dissolved nutrients are hidden in tubes. This saves them the effort of growing their own roots to find their own supplies. Some parasitic plants can also make their own food by creating sugars through the process of photosynthesis in their hosts' leaves, even if only for part of their life cycle. However, most just take what they need.

A Stringy Parasite

Dodder is a plant that resembles long strands of string or even spaghetti. It has no leaves, or only tiny ones, and cannot make enough food to survive. So it grows upward and twines around, between, and over other plants. The dodder pushes out parts, called haustoria, from its stem, which burrow into another plant's flesh to feed on the nutrients inside.

Extreme!

Dodder Dawn

Some dodder species can produce over 16,000 seeds per plant, and these can survive for up to 60 years in the soil. Once the soil is moist enough and the sun is shining, each seed sprouts roots and a thin yellow stem that grows upward. The stem then gropes in the air until it makes contact with a host. After the plant starts to feed, the roots rot away as they are no longer necessary.

Dodder can take over and damage whole fields of crops by twining around and feeding on its hosts.

Corpse Flower

The biggest flower in the world is a parasite. Each single red-and-white spotted bloom measures 3 feet (1 m) across and smells of dead, rotting flesh. This is the corpse flower, or *rafflesia arnoldii*, that grows in the rain forests of Borneo, in Southeast Asia.

Vine Invader

The corpse flower spends most of its life out of sight, living inside the stem or roots of woody vines running under the forest floor. It only becomes visible when flower buds start to sprout from the ground like dark mushrooms. These soon open, and flowers begin to swell and grow. They look like no other flowers on Earth. They are fleshy and resemble red tires with five large lobes around them. Bizarre!

Only about one-tenth of rafflesia flower buds actually open into a flower, and there are more male than female flowers.

Foul Flower

At the heart of each bloom is a column, carrying a disk with male or female parts. The bloom warms and starts to create an appalling stench. Flies hurry to the flower to climb inside, in search of what they think is rotting flesh. As they crawl around, they rub pollen from male parts onto female parts, and the rafflesia starts to make seeds.

Millions of seeds stay in the soil after a corpse flower bloom fades, but few survive.

Extreme!

Sleeping Gas

The corpse flower creates heat. This helps make the chemicals that smell of death spread through the air. The heat is also a result of the rafflesia flower producing lots of carbon dioxide gas. This can help make visiting flies drowsy so that they stick around in the flower long enough to pollinate it.

Australian Christmas Tree

The giant of the parasitic plant world is the Australian Christmas tree, which stands 30 feet (9 m) tall. When young, this plant fends for itself, making food by photosynthesis and getting nutrients from the soil. When it grows into an adult, the plant latches onto other nearby plants to get the nutrients it needs.

Attractive Assassin

In western Australia, the dry season happens around Christmas. Yet it is not uncommon at this time to spot a beautiful tree thickly coated in yellow and orange flowers, surrounded by other plants that look dry and almost dead. This is the Australian Christmas tree, and it thrives by killing its neighbors, tapping into their roots to steal water and nutrients. The trees assassinate anything from grasses to shrubs.

The roots of the Australian Christmas tree can spread 300 feet (90 m) in every direction to grab onto plants all around.

The Australian Christmas tree can put on a fine flower display only because it is attacking other plants underground.

What Lies Beneath

The Australian Christmas tree's long, widespread roots grow and creep unseen underground until they reach a host root. Then the tip of the parasite's root forms a white ring around the host root. In the ring, there is a sharp, scissor-shaped part that slices into the host root to connect with the tubes inside, which carry water and nutrients. It is then a simple matter for the parasite to redirect the nourishing flow into its own roots.

Extra Extreme

The Australian Christmas tree is a close relative of mistletoe, which grows on trees such as oak. Birds feed on mistletoe berries, and the sticky seeds inside stick to their beaks. When they fly to another tree and wipe their beaks on a branch, the seeds may start growing there.

Chapter 4

Stingers and Stabbers

Plants have many different ways of stopping large animals from damaging or eating them. Among the most extreme are the stabbers and stingers. These vicious plants have jagged thorns or sharp spikes that deter would-be attackers, or they contain nasty substances that can sting and burn.

Stinging Nettles

The leaves and stems of a stinging nettle are covered with tiny hairs. Each one of these hairs can deliver a painful sting. This keeps most grazing animals away. Small insects are unaffected. They land on the plants to feed and then carry pollen to other stinging nettles, where they help its flowers make seeds that grow into new plants.

Some small animals can touch stinging nettles without getting stung—unlike us.

Nasty Needles

The hairs on a stinging nettle are like hollow tubes, with walls made from a glass-like substance called silica. Inside these tiny needles is a stinging liquid that contains formic acid and other nasty chemicals. When an animal brushes against the glassy hairs, their tips break off to leave a sharp point that injects the skin with the painful potion.

The hairs on a stinging nettle act like hypodermic needles to deliver their stinging fluid.

Extra Extreme

The stinging nettle is not the only plant that delivers a nasty sting. People have described being stung by the Australian gympie-gympie stinging tree as the worst kind of pain you can imagine—like being burned with hot acid and electrocuted at the same time! The venomous hairs that cover this plant's stems, leaves, and fruits pose a danger to walkers and workers who dare to venture into the rain forests where these plants grow.

Whistling Thorn Acacia

On the open savannah of Kenya, where the whistling thorn acacia tree grows, there are several large animals with big appetites that would love to feast on this plant's leaves and twigs. They have no chance! This smart tree has big thorns containing very special bodyguards to protect it from the unwanted attentions of large browsers such as giraffes and elephants.

Double Thorns

The whistling thorn acacia protects itself with pairs of long, fiercely sharp thorns up to 3 inches (8 cm) long. If an animal rubs too closely against these vicious-looking weapons, it will get a nasty cut. At the base of each pair of thorns is another dangerous surprise: hollow areas about 1 inch (2.5 cm) wide that contain hoards of stinging ants.

Thorns alone do not deter giraffes. Giraffes have long, flexible tongues that can wrap around the soft leaves and pull them off without touching the thorns.

The ants make tiny holes in the swollen thorns to get in and out of their nests. Wind blowing through the holes makes a whistling sound.

Bodyguard Ants

Different kinds of stinging ants make their nests inside the swollen base of the thorns and feed on nectar from the lower part of the acacia's leaves. To protect their homes and food supply, the ants will swarm out of their nests and attack any animals that brush against the tree or try to eat parts of it. Of course, this also protects the tree.

Extreme!

Scent Trails

When ants leave their nests in search of food, they leave a scent trail to tell other ants where they are going. Scientists think that giraffes and some other browsing animals can smell the scents that ants give off to communicate with each other, and this warns the big browsers to leave the whistling thorn acacia trees alone.

Puya

On the plains and foothills of the mountains of Chile in South America lives a highly unusual plant called puya, which uses daggerlike spikes to stab animals that get too close. A range of wildlife has met a grisly end because of this plant, including birds and even sheep.

Brutal Blades

The puya's deadly weapons are found at the end of its leaves, where there are hard, outward-pointing spikes. Animals get caught on and entangled by these spikes and cannot escape. After the animals have died, their bodies decay and decompose. This releases nutrients from the animal's body into the ground around the plant. These animal remains act as a gruesome fertilizer to nourish this wonder plant and help it grow.

The tall, spiky puya plant is named for the Mapuche Indian word for "point."

Extreme!

Rare Blossoms

The puya plant does not have a long time to reproduce. It flowers just once every 15 to 20 years and remains in bloom for only about a week. Perhaps that is why it uses its spikes like a barbed-wire fence to protect the flowers and give small birds a chance to pollinate it.

Fatal Flowers

Experts believe that the spikes are there mainly to stop animals from reaching the center of the plant, where the flowers grow. The puya plant grows a gigantic tower of chunky, colorful flowers that can reach up to 10 feet (3 m) tall. The flowers are bright blue-green with deep-orange stamens covered in pollen. Small birds visit the flowers to feed on nectar, and they help pollinate the plant.

The flowers on a puya flower tower are up to 2 inches (5 cm) long and contain enough nectar for a person to drink!

Chapter 5

Home Wreckers

Some plants are home wreckers. They may take over a small space or a large area and, in the process, harm or kill other plants and sometimes animals that live there. These plants are not being mean. They are attempting to survive and thrive in their shared habitat or environment.

Race for Space

The living things that normally inhabit a particular place are all in competition with each other. They are not competing for prizes or world records but rather resources. These are the things they need to survive. Plants must have space to grow because they need access to the water, nutrients, and sunlight that are vital for making food so they can grow and remain healthy.

When farmers spill fertilizers and animal manure into water, they increase the nutrient resources for algae, which then often multiply.

Extra Extreme

Some algal blooms are deadly because each of their cells makes a tiny amount of poison. Together in a bloom, the algae create a sinister soup. This may poison any animal that drinks the water or eats smaller animals that have been feeding in it.

Blooming Algae

Algae are plantlike organisms that make their own food by photosynthesis, as true plants do. Algae live in water. Sometimes there are lots of nutrients in the water, which makes the algae grow and reproduce fast. This is called an algal bloom. The algae take up space from and smother other plants. Algae live short lives, and as more grow, more die. As a result, more bacteria thrive in the water because they feed by breaking down dead algae. This process uses up oxygen dissolved in the water, so fish and other water animals cannot breathe.

Fish die in some algal blooms because of the poisons they take in from the algae but also because the algae clog their gills.

Strangler Fig

Have you ever seen a picture of a ruined temple in a rain forest with tree roots entwined and growing over its surface? These trees are called strangler figs, or banyans. They look pretty but are notorious tree killers. As their name suggests, these creeping killers strangle their victims to death.

Young Criminals

Strangler figs begin their life of crime high up, as epiphytes. These are plants that grow on the branches of other plants, particularly trees. The young seedlings then get busy. They produce lots of long roots that grow down a tree trunk and dig into the ground. The young strangler then has growth spurts as it takes in nutrients and water from the soil. All the roots grow thicker and merge together, forming a network around the tree.

The strangler fig grows wide buttress roots to support it in its fight to survive.

Death Grip

The root network grips the tree tighter and tighter. It squeezes the trunk tightly enough to stop water and nutrients from flowing up inside. The death grip is only part of the strangler fig's scheme. High in the tree, it also grows lots of branches covered with leaves that block light from getting to the leaves of the tree itself. Eventually the tree dies and rots away, leaving just the triumphant fig.

The rotting wood in the center of a successful strangler fig (left over from the tree it killed) is a useful source of nutrients.

Extreme!

Figs for Food

The fig trees in rain forests are keystone species, which means they help many other species survive. Fig trees produce fruit several times a year that forest animals such as monkeys and parrots eat. These animals are then vital foods for predators, including jaguars and harpy eagles.

Black Walnut Tree

The black walnut tree of North America is a giant. Some plants cannot grow beneath or even near it because this mighty colossus blocks out the light and sucks up lots of water through its roots. There is also another good reason why few plants live nearby—the black walnut poisons them!

Black walnut trees can reach heights of 150 feet (45 m) and grow a spread of branches 100 feet (30 m) all around.

Poisonous Peril

The chemical made by the black walnut that poisons other plants is called juglone. Juglone works by blocking the tubes that transport water through plants, which prevents them from taking in carbon dioxide and oxygen gases. Juglone acts fast. A plant can change from healthy to dead in two days. The symptoms of walnut poisoning include stunted growth, yellowing leaves, and wilting.

Plants that are sensitive to juglone poisoning include tomatoes, potatoes, and apple trees.

Persistent Protection

The black walnut produces juglone for protection. The chemical helps stop insects and other animals from eating its parts and helps prevent other plants from competing for space and nutrients. The juglone moves through the tree to maximize protection. In spring, lots of it is found in the tender leaves the tree must protect to carry out photosynthesis. In the summer, juglone moves to the roots to keep other plants away and make sure the tree can drink at the driest time of year.

Extreme!

Bed of Poison

Juglone hangs around even when a black walnut tree has been cut down. It can take six months for the remaining roots, bark, or woodchips to stop being poisonous. A horse can become sick if black walnut chips that still contain juglone are used in its bedding.

Chapter 6

Deadly Dinners

We all know how important it is to eat a wide range of fruits and vegetables, but did you also know that some of the food plants we eat have parts that are actually poisonous? Plants have poisoned parts to keep animals from eating them—and it usually works.

Rhubarb Leaves

The reason that stores sell rhubarb with its leaves cut off is because rhubarb leaves, whether they are raw or cooked, contain dangerously high levels of poison. If you eat too many leaves, it can cause serious kidney damage—and even kill you. This rarely happens now because we know about the dangers. Also, you would need to eat a huge amount of the bitter-tasting leaves to die. However, even a small amount can make you sick.

Rhubarb leaves are deadly, but the cooked stems are full of nutrients.

Kidney Beans

Chili would not taste nearly as good without kidney beans—but never ever try to eat them raw. Raw kidney beans taste bad and are hard to chew, but worse than that, they contain natural toxins called lectins that can cause extreme nausea, vomiting, and an upset stomach. To avoid these horrors, it is vital to soak raw red kidney beans in water for at least five hours and then boil them at high heat until they are soft.

Extra Extreme

The mushrooms you buy in a store are safe and good to eat, but avoid picking wild mushrooms, many of which are toxic. One of the deadliest is the aptly named death cap mushroom. It does not look dangerous and is said to taste good, but just a few bites are enough to kill a human.

Do not eat mushrooms from the wild, unless an adult says they are safe. They could be deadly, like these death caps.

Castor Oil Plant

People press the seeds of the castor oil plant to extract its oil, which has a number of different uses. The oil is said to help treat fungal infections on the skin and to soothe eyes and joint pain. It is also added to candies, chocolate, and other foods. These seeds have to be handled with care, however, because they are among the deadliest on Earth.

Beating the Insects

The castor oil plant is native to Africa, but people have planted it all over because it is both attractive and tough. It has clusters of flowers that produce prickly fruits. When the fruits are ripe, they explode and spray the seeds inside them all around to spread the plant to new places. All parts of the castor oil plant are poisonous, which protects it against insect pests such as aphids—but it is the seeds that are the most dangerous.

The shiny, mottled seeds of the castor oil plant look attractive, but they are deadly. It only takes one or two seeds to kill a child and up to eight to kill an adult.

The castor oil plant can reach heights of nearly 15 feet (4.5 m) when it grows in warm, damp, open spaces.

Seeds of Death

Castor oil seeds contain a deadly toxin called ricin. The animals most at risk from this poison are cattle, horses, sheep, pigs, and rabbits. The symptoms of poisoning by ricin are nausea, vomiting, stomach pains, headaches, diarrhea, fever, and seizures, followed eventually by death. Understandably, this keeps animals from eating castor oil seeds! The seeds then have a chance to sink into the soil, where they can sprout and develop—known as germination—and grow into new plants.

Extreme!

Oil for Mummies

About half the weight of the castor oil seed is made up of the thick, almost colorless oil that people have used for centuries. Ancient Egyptians used castor oil for their lamps and as an ointment. Castor oil seeds that are thousands of years old have even been found in the stone coffins, known as sarcophagi, of these ancient people, who believed the seeds might be useful in the afterlife.

Cassava

Cyanide is one of the most deadly poisons in the world. It can cause anything from headaches and dizziness to comas and brain disease. One of the plants that produces cyanide is cassava. Yet this killer plant is an important food and major source of nutrition for half a billion people around the globe.

Fiendish Food

In parts of Africa, Asia, and South America, people eat cassava roots, known as tubers, because they contain large amounts of starch, a type of carbohydrate that helps fill them up and supplies sugars for nutrition. People generally avoid the leaves, which release cyanide when eaten. Cassava makes the poison not only to deter people but also animals such as insects and rats.

The root of the cassava plant contains not only starch but also other nutrients, including calcium and vitamin C.

Cassava can be cooked in different ways, after it is boiled to make it safe, including frying in oil to make tasty fries.

Destroying the Danger

People always process cassava before eating it to destroy its ability to release cyanide. The less potent sweet cassava is dried in the sun for days or simply boiled. Dealing with bitter cassava is much more time-consuming. People need to wash the peeled tubers, grate them to a pulp, squeeze the pulp, sieve it, and then soak the remains in water for days before roasting. The dried remains then need to be cooked before they are safe.

Extreme!

Kill or Cure?

Raw cassava does not contain cyanide but makes it. When animals and people chew cassava, this breaks down the plant cell walls and unleashes a chemical called linamarase, which is able to change other chemicals into cyanide. Scientists are trying to treat cancer by using linamarase to produce cyanide that zaps only cancer cells, and not healthy ones.

Chapter 7

Warning Signs

Most of the world's creeping killer plants use thorns, toxins, or other extreme tactics to harm fellow living things as a means of defense. These defense tactics stop other organisms from damaging and eating the plants, or prevent them from reproducing. Many of these plants also have ways to warn animals that they are dangerous even before animals bite or touch them.

Red for Danger

Some plants grow highly visible, long, sharp thorns. Others display warning colors. Rosary peas are bright red, which is a color often used in nature as a danger sign. These peas contain abrin, an extremely deadly poison. They were named for their use in strings of rosary beads and have also been used in jewelry. Unfortunately, many jewelry makers in the past did not heed the warning signs and became sick or died after working with rosary peas.

Some seeds, such as these rosary peas, have bold warning colors to tell animals to avoid them.

Strange Sap

Other plants use bad tastes and smells, or strange milky-looking sap, to deter would-be diners. Euphorbia plants have a highly toxic, milky sap. The sap helps seal wounds if the plant stems get broken, and it has antibacterial properties that stop the plant from getting infected with diseases. The sap looks unpleasant, which warns animals that it is highly irritating and will give them a nasty burning sensation on their skin if they harm the plant.

Extra Extreme

Not all toxic creeping killers give warnings. The oleander is a beautiful plant with colorful flowers and soft leaves. However, it is highly toxic if eaten and can irritate the skin if handled. All parts of an oleander are poisonous, so do not touch! Avoid any unfamiliar plants—in case they are one of nature's deadly creeping killers!

Oleanders are beautiful, but appearances can be deceiving. Even burning this deadly plant can be toxic and very irritating.

Glossary

bacteria single-celled living things, some of which can be harmful

bulb an underground bud protected by thick, fleshy leaves

carbohydrate a food type that is a source of energy for our bodies

carnivorous describes a plant or animal that feeds on animals

cells the microscopically small building blocks of living things

digest to break down food inside the body to get nutrients from it

enzyme a substance that helps chemical reactions happen inside the bodies of living things

epiphyte a plant that grows high up on a tree to reach light

fertilizer a substance people use to improve plant growth

fruit the part of a plant that contains and protects its seeds

germination the process where a seed starts to sprout and develop

gills the body parts that allow aquatic animals to breathe in water

gland an organ in the body with a particular job to do, such as make sweat or release substances called hormones that tell the body how to work and how to grow

habitat the environment in which animals and plants live

host an animal or plant on which a parasite lives

immune resistant to or protected against a disease or danger

nectar the sugary substance found in plants

nutrients the chemicals that nourish living things and help them live and grow

paralyze to cause something to be wholly or partly incapable of movement

photosynthesis the process by which a plant makes its own food

pollen a powder made by the male part of a flower

pollinate what happens when pollen travels from one flower to another and causes seeds to grow there

predator an animal that catches and eats other animals

prey an animal that is caught and eaten by other animals

reproduce to have offspring

resources things that can be used or have value, such as oil

root a plant part that grows underground

sap a sugary liquid containing food made in a plant's leaves

species a type of living thing

stamen the part of a flower that produces pollen

stem the part of the plant that holds it upright and supports its flowers and leaves

toxin a poison

For More Information

Books

Aaseng, Nathan. *Weird Meat-Eating Plants* (Bizarre Science). Berkeley Heights, NJ: Enslow Publishers, Inc., 2011.

Burnie, David. *Plant* (DK Eyewitness Books). New York, NY: DK Publishing, 2011.

Waldron, Melanie. *Plants* (Essential Life Science). North Mankato, MN: Heinemann InfoSearch, 2014.

Zuchora-Walske, Christine. *Photosynthesis* (The Science of Life). Minneapolis, MN: ABDO Publishing, 2014.

Websites

There are lots of fun facts about plants at:
www.sciencekids.co.nz/sciencefacts/plants.html

Find out more about carnivorous plants at:
kids.nationalgeographic.com/kids/stories/animalsnature/meat-eating-plants

Publisher's note to educators and parents: Our editors have carefully reviewed these websites to ensure that they are suitable for students. Many websites change frequently, however, and we cannot guarantee that a site's future contents will continue to meet our high standards of quality and educational value. Be advised that students should be closely supervised whenever they access the Internet.

Index